The *Monitor* National Marine Sanctuary
Revised Management Plan

REVISED DRAFT

November 1996

Sanctuaries and Reserves Division
Office of Ocean and Coastal Resource Management
National Ocean Service
National Oceanic and Atmospheric Administration
U.S. Department of Commerce

Executive Summary

On January 30, 1975, NOAA designated the wreck of the USS *Monitor*, lying off the coast of North Carolina, as the Nation's first marine sanctuary. The *Monitor* was the prototype for a class of U.S. Civil War ironclad, turreted warships that significantly altered both naval technology and marine architecture in the nineteenth century. Designed by the Swedish-American engineer John Ericsson, the vessel contained all of the emerging innovations that revolutionized warfare at sea.

The *Monitor*'s career as a warship was significant, though short-lived. On March 9, 1862, she battled the CSS *Virginia* (ex-USS *Merrimack*) in one of the most celebrated naval battles in history. On December 25, 1862, the ironclad received orders to proceed, under tow, to Beaufort, North Carolina. En route, the *Monitor* encountered a severe gale and began to take on water. On December 31, 1862, less than a year after her commissioning, the *Monitor* sank with a loss of sixteen men.

For over a century the *Monitor* lay undiscovered. In August, 1973, scientists aboard Duke University's research vessel *Eastward* located the *Monitor* in 230 feet of water, 16 miles off Cape Hatteras, North Carolina. The wreck was in generally good condition, although some structural damage and deterioration was apparent.

Numerous research expeditions have visited the *Monitor* National Marine Sanctuary. The anchor, a signal lantern, and more than one hundred other artifacts have been recovered and many are on display at The Mariners' Museum in Newport News, Virginia, the principal museum for the Sanctuary. Traveling and temporary exhibits have also been displayed at various museums, conferences and special events.

Announcements of the *Monitor*'s discovery stimulated considerable interest in the wreck. Today the *Monitor* represents a unique legacy from our Nation's past. The shipwreck and its contents comprise an irreplaceable historical record and represent a monument to the American naval tradition that the vessel itself helped to create.

Archaeological investigations of the *Monitor* can provide an opportunity to examine aspects of our past that are not recorded in surviving manuscript sources. Artifacts from the ship's stores and personal property of the crew can greatly enhance our understanding of life aboard the United States Navy's first ironclad warship.

This revised management plan provides an integrated program of resource protection, research, education and interpretation. The plan outlines comprehensive management objectives that have been revised and expanded, based upon new knowledge of the site and upon new opportunities for research and education. This plan defines a framework for continued resource protection and preservation, as well as for an expanded program of on-site research that will contribute to the basic store of knowledge regarding this unique resource. This expanding data base will aid NOAA in determining the proper eventual disposition of the wreck. The plan calls for the establishment of partnerships with other governmental and private organizations who share an interest in the *Monitor*.

This management plan also provides for an expanded education program for the Sanctuary. Since it is impossible for most people to visit the site, an effective, innovative education program offers an opportunity to "bring the *Monitor* to the public" through such means as lectures, films, interactive CD-ROM programs and exhibits. The education program also addresses the need to inform the site's users of the *Monitor*'s significance in order to limit inadvertent damage to the wreck. To reinforce these education efforts and to further protect the site, the plan outlines NOAA's agreement with the U.S. Coast Guard for enforcement of the Sanctuary's regulations. Lastly, this plan outlines options for increasing access to the Sanctuary for non-research purposes.

Public comments were received for this management plan in 1992, but the plan was not published until 1995 due to the need for further on-site research. This plan replaces the 1983 management plan for the Sanctuary, setting forth management policies for the *Monitor* that recognize its importance as an irreplaceable cultural resource and as a National Marine Sanctuary. The management plan will be updated as needed.

Contents

Introduction

The National Marine Sanctuary Program

The Marine Protection, Research, and Sanctuaries Act of 1972 (16 U.S.C. 1431) (MPRSA), authorizes the Secretary of Commerce to designate discrete areas as National Marine Sanctuaries in order to promote comprehensive management of their special ecological, historical, recreational, and aesthetic resources. National Marine Sanctuaries may be designated in coastal and ocean waters, in submerged lands, and in the Great Lakes and their connecting waters. The MPRSA is administered by the National Oceanic and Atmospheric Administration (NOAA) through the Office of Ocean and Coastal Resource Management's Sanctuaries and Reserves Division (SRD).

Program Goals

The SRD's goal is to establish a system of National Marine Sanctuaries based on the identification, designation, and comprehensive management of special marine areas for the long-term protection and use of resources by the public. The overall goals of the National Marine Sanctuary Program are to:

Enhance resource protection through comprehensive and coordinated conservation and management of Sanctuary resources that complement existing regulatory authorities;

Support, promote, coordinate, and conduct scientific research and monitoring of marine resources to improve the management in National Marine Sanctuaries;

Enhance public awareness, understanding, and wise use of the marine environment through public interpretive, educational, and recreational program; and

Facilitate, to the extent compatible with the primary objective of resource protection, multiple uses of National Marine Sanctuaries.

The Sanctuaries

Twelve National Marine Sanctuaries have been established since the Program's inception in 1972. They include near-shore coral reefs and open ocean, and range in size from less than one to more than 4000 square nautical miles. The Sanctuaries harbor a fascinating array of plants and animals, from whales to brightly colored sea snails. In many cases, these protected waters provide a secure habitat for species close to extinction. Some of the Sanctuaries protect significant historical and cultural resources, as well as natural resources.

Many of the Sanctuaries are also cherished recreational spots for diving and fishing in addition to supporting valuable commercial industries, such as the harvesting of fish and kelp. A major part of the challenge of managing these areas is balancing compatible multiple uses of the resources. These Sanctuaries are a public trust to be managed for the use and enjoyment of present and future generations.

The following descriptions of the existing National Marine Sanctuaries (NMS) are given in the order of their designation:

- The *Monitor* NMS protects the wreck of the Civil War ironclad USS *Monitor*. It was Designated in January, 1975, the was the nation's first marine sanctuary. The sanctuary is 1 nautical mile in diameter and is located 16.1 miles southeast of Cape Hatteras, North Carolina.

- The **Channel Islands** NMS encompasses 1,252 square miles off the coast of Santa Barbara, California. The Sanctuary surrounds the four northern Channel Islands and Santa Barbara Island, and protects valuable habitats for marine mammals, including seals and seabirds.

- The **Gray's Reef** NMS is a submerged live bottom area located on the South Atlantic continental shelf due east of Sapelo Island, Georgia. The Sanctuary encompasses 17 square miles and protects a highly productive and unusual habitat for a wide variety of species including corals, invertebrates, and endangered and threatened sea turtles.

- The **Gulf of the Farallones** NMS encompasses 948 square miles off the northern coast of San Francisco, California. The Sanctuary includes important habitats for a diverse array of marine mammals and seabirds, as well as ocean-dwelling (pelagic) fish, plants, and bottom-dwelling (benthic) organisms.

- The **Fagetele Bay** NMS in American Samoa is a 163-acre bay site containing deep-water coral terrace formations unique to the high islands of the tropical Pacific. The Sanctuary protects habitat for a diverse array of marine flora and fauna, including the endangered hawksbill sea turtle and the threatened green sea turtle.

- The **Cordell Bank** NMS, lies offshore in California. The 397-square-mile site surrounds a granite formation which provides habitat for an unusual assortment of marine and intertidal species, including colonies of purple hydrocorals. Abundant fish species attract feeding seabirds and cetaceans (whales, porpoises and dolphins).

- The **Florida Keys** NMS was Congressionally designated in November, 1990, and encompasses approximately 2,600 square miles of coral reefs, seagrass beds, and related shoreline habitats off Florida. The Florida Keys NMS subsumes the previously-designated Key Largo NMS and the Looe Key NMS. The Key Largo section provides protection and management to a 100-square-mile area of tropical coral reefs south of Miami, Florida, and is a seaward extension of the John Pennekamp State Coral Reef Park. The Looe Key section consists of a submerged section of the Florida reef southwest of Big Pine Key and includes a beautiful "spur and groove: coral formation supporting a diverse marine community.

- The **Flower Garden Banks** NMS encompasses 42 square miles surrounding the East and West Flower Garden Banks, situated over 100 miles off the coast of Texas. The Sanctuary protects the northernmost coral reefs on the North American continental shelf.

- The **Monterey Bay** NMS is the largest Sanctuary at 4,024 square nautical miles. Designated in September 1992, this productive environment supports a diverse biological community of both warm- and cold-water organisms. The most prominent feature of the Sanctuary is a spectacular nearshore submarine canyon.

- The **Hawaiian Islands Humpback Whale** NMS includes waters surrounding Maui, Lanai Molokai, and part of Kauai. This habitat is a breeding and calving area for humpback whales.

- The **Stellwagen Banks** NMS is located 25 miles east of Boston, Massachusetts. This glacially deposited submerged sand bank supports large population of fish and marine mammals. At least eight species of marine mammals use the bank as a nursery and feeding ground during seasonal migrations.

- The **Olympic Coast** NMS is located adjacent to the Pacific coast of Washington State. Designated in June 1994, the area is inhabited by numerous endangered of threatened species including bald eagles, peregrine falcons, brown pelicans, gray, blue, and humpback whales, and harbor porpoises. Salmon, shellfish, and bottom-dwelling fishes such as halibut and cod are the mainstays of the commercial and recreational fisheries.

- ***Proposed Sanctuaries:*** The Division is currently preparing designation documents for two additional proposed Sanctuaries: Northwest Straits, Washington and Thunder Bay, Michigan.

The *Monitor* National Marine Sanctuary

The USS *Monitor* was designed by John Ericsson, a Swedish-American engineer, and was built at Greenpoint, Long Island, at a total cost of $275,000. The *Monitor* was the prototype for a new class of American ironclads. Among her many unique features were a revolving gun turret, an anchor that could be raised and lowered from below deck, forced-air ventilation, and a flushing shipboard toilet. Her first battle, on March 9, 1862 at Hampton Roads, Virginia, was with the Confederate ironclad ram CSS *Virginia* (ex-*Merrimack*). The battle between the *Monitor and Merrim*ack, the first confrontation between ironclad warships, was one of the most celebrated naval battles in American history, changing forever the course of naval warfare and setting a totally new direction in naval architecture and ship design.

Eleven months after being launched, the *Monitor*'s promising career was cut short. The *Monitor* and 16 of her crew were lost while under tow by the vessel USS *Rhode Island* off of Cape Hatteras, North Carolina, an area known as the "Graveyard of the Atlantic." The ironclad, unable to weather the heavy gale-driven seas, foundered and sank on December 31, 1862.

The *Monitor*'s final resting place in the Atlantic Ocean remained unknown for more than a century. A number of unsuccessful searches for the wreck took place after World War II.

Finally, in August 1973, scientists conducting a project using side-scan sonar onboard the R/V *Eastward* located the *Monitor*'s remains and obtained the first video of the wreckage using remotely operated still and video cameras. A second expedition to the site in April, 1974, aboard the research vessel *Alcoa Seaprobe*, verified the ship's identity and produced a photomosaic of the wreck.

Sanctuary Designation

The discovery of the *Monitor* was announced jointly by Duke University and the North Carolina Department of Archives and History on March 7, 1974. A question was immediately posed: What should be done with one of the most important objects — both symbolically and actually — in American history? After many discussions among a wide variety of Federal, state and local organizations as well as historians and the public, the Governor of North Carolina nominated the wreck of the *Monitor* for National Marine Sanctuary status on September 26, 1974. To further the cause of protecting this valuable historic resource, the Secretary of the Interior listed the USS *Monitor* on the National Register of Historic Places on October 11, 1974.

On January 30, 1975, the Secretary of Commerce made history when he designated the remains of the USS *Monitor* and a column of water one mile surrounding the vessel as the Nation's first marine sanctuary.

On March 9, 1987, the 125th anniversary of the *Monitor-Virginia* battle, the Secretary of the Interior, Donald Hodel, designated the USS *Monitor* as a National Historic Landmark.

Goals and Objectives

Sanctuary goals and objectives provide the framework for developing management strategies. The goals and objectives direct Sanctuary activities which address the dual purposes of resource protection and multiple use, and are consistent with the intent of the National Marine Sanctuary Program.

Management strategies for the *Monitor* NMS focus on the goals and objectives outlined in this section. While these goals and objectives are listed separately, their effects overlap. Resource protection efforts, for instance, include expanding the Sanctuary's education program.

Resource Protection

Title III of the MPRSA authorizes NOAA to manage sanctuaries' historical resources, among others. In doing so, the agency must comply with the Federal Archaeological Program as outlined in Executive Order 11593 and Federal statutes defined in the National Historic Preservation Act of 1966 (NHPA) and the Archaeological Resources Protection Act of 1979 (ARPA), as well as those acts' implementing regulations.

NOAA had no existing historical/cultural resources management policy when the USS. *Monitor* was designated as the first National Marine Sanctuary in 1975. Since the *Monitor* was one of the most significant historic shipwrecks in U.S. waters, a special policy was adopted for that site (Title III, sec. 314 added by PL 100-627, MPRSA). SRD has since published a comprehensive historical context study and resources policy that address the historic and cultural resources of all of the National Marine Sanctuaries (Terrell, 1994).

The highest priority management goal for the *Monitor* Sanctuary is resource protection through comprehensive and coordinated conservation and management of the wreck and its surroundings. An important part of our Nation's history, the *Monitor*, its artifacts, the archaeological information at the site, the archaeological collection and the *Monitor*'s records are all part of the Sanctuary's resources. Specific major objectives of the resource protection program are to:

- Continue the current cooperative program with the U. S. Coast Guard for surveillance of the site and enforcement of Sanctuary regulations;

- Promote public awareness of, and voluntary user compliance with, Sanctuary regulations through an education program stressing the site's sensitivity to human disturbances;

- Continue the current program of monitoring studies to document and analyze changes to the *Monitor* and its immediate environment;

- Evaluate technologies and resources for stabilization of the *Monitor*, including cathodic protection and physical supports; and

- Map and recover *Monitor* artifacts which are in danger of being damaged or destroyed; transport them to The Mariners' Museum in Newport News, Virginia, the principal museum for the *Monitor* NMS, where they will be conserved and placed into the *Monitor* Collection for permanent curation, exhibit and research.

Research

The *Monitor* Sanctuary requires a research program that addresses resource protection as well as other management issues. Initial research supported by NOAA was directed primarily toward protection through a comprehensive site characterization process that increased our understanding of the *Monitor's* remains and how they have been affected by natural deterioration and human activities. This research was critical to developing effective approaches to long-range management issues.

NOAA's initial site characterization research and recent monitoring and research activities by NOAA and private researchers, resulted in the detection of a significant increase in the rate of deterioration of the *Monitor*. The rapid degradation of the hull, as described later in this document, may have been precipitated by an incident in 1991 when a private fishing boat was cited by the Coast Guard for anchoring illegally on the wreck. It is also possible, however, that the structural integrity of the *Monitor* has decreased through natural deterioration to the point that the rate of collapse has begun to accelerate.

As a result of this new information, current research goals for the *Monitor* Sanctuary are to ensure the scientific recovery and dissemination of historical and cultural information from the site, and to preserve and manage the remains of the *Monitor* in a manner that appropriately enhances both the significance and interpretive potential of the warship.

Specific objectives of the revised research program include:

- Continue the conduct of baseline and monitoring studies to aid in determining the rate of change of the ship, as well as changes in the Sanctuary environment;

- Conduct additional predictive studies to assess causes and effects of corrosion, environmental conditions, and human activities and to anticipate management issues;

- Continue to assess possible options for stabilizing the *Monitor* through physical supports, cathodic protection or other means;

- Conduct additional archaeological investigations for the purposes of further documenting the wreck and recovering additional cultural information and artifacts; and

- Encourage increased public and private participation in *Monitor* research.

Education

The education program is directed to enhancing public awareness and understanding of the significance of the Sanctuary and the need to protect the *Monitor*. Specific objectives of the education program are to:

- Maintain the *Monitor* Collection and promote its use for education and research;

- Provide the public with information on the *Monitor* and its surroundings, with emphasis on the need to protect the wreck and its artifacts;

- Enhance and broaden support for the Sanctuary and Sanctuary management by offering programs and printed materials suited to audiences with a range of interests and backgrounds;

- Encourage research and information exchange among parties interested in the *Monitor;*

- Promote public and private participation in *Monitor* education programs.

Special Uses

Monitor Sanctuary regulations state that research is the only allowable site activity. Therefore, proposals for non-research diving activities have routinely been denied by NOAA, due to concerns for possible damage to the wreck and its contents as well as for possible diver injuries, since the wreck is well below the depth normally considered safe for scuba diving. However, during the public review of the draft of this revised management plan, NOAA received several well-presented comments from divers asking NOAA to reconsider the public access issue in light of recent improvements in the techniques and equipment for deep diving.

As a result, NOAA delayed issue of the management plan until the public access issue could be reassessed. First, NOAA reviewed the safety record of private divers who had conducted permitted research at the Sanctuary since 1990. After several hundred self-contained air and mixed-gas dives to the *Monitor*, no serious injuries were reported. Then, in 1994, through a competitive request for proposals, NOAA issued a special use permit to a private charter boat captain for the conduct of non-research dives on the *Monitor*.

NOAA concluded that recent advances in deep diving (often referred to as "technical diving") make it feasible to allow increased non-research access, which will be accomplished through special use permits.

The *Monitor*'s remains lie on the Continental Shelf 16.1 nautical miles south-southeast of the Cape Hatteras Lighthouse. The *Monitor* Sanctuary consists of a vertical column of water in the Atlantic Ocean one mile in diameter extending from the surface to the seabed. The center of the water column is 35°00'23" north latitude and 75°24'32" west longitude.

In the vicinity of the *Monitor*, the ocean bottom is composed of sand, shell hash, and clay below the surface. Bathymetric profiles (topography of the sea floor) of the area indicate that the bottom surface slopes gently away to the southeast at less than seven feet per 1000 feet.

Visibility. Visibility in the 230-foot-deep water varies according to turbidity, the presence of microorganisms, and the intensity and angle of sunlight. Records to date indicate that visibility varies from approximately 10 feet to more than 150 feet.

Currents. The site lies at the western margin of the Gulf Stream, and the area is influenced both by the Stream itself and by eddies created by that current. Changes in current direction and velocity occur frequently. Within a 24-hour period, direction has been observed to change 360 degrees. Current velocities are known to vary from zero to more than 1.5 knots at the bottom, and surface currents can be considerably stronger. Water temperature in the area seems to be related to these current patterns. While few specific data are available, temperature projections indicate an annual variation between 52 degrees and 78 degrees Fahrenheit.

Wind patterns. In the area of the Sanctuary, wind patterns can be generalized as prevailing from the north to west between November and February; north-northwest and south-southwest between March and June; south-southeast during July and August; and north-northeast during September and October. However, unpredictable variations are common and spontaneous storms frequently occur.

Biological organisms. A biological study carried out by NOAA in June 1990 identified encrusting organisms and motile invertebrates on the wreck (Table 1). The wide variety of encrusting organisms included coral, sponges, sea squirts, sea anemones, hydroids, barnacles, tube worms, mussels, and oysters. *Oculina arbuscula* was the most abundant coral, but at least 40 species of sponges were observed. Although many invertebrates are cryptic and hard to detect, those identified were crabs, brittlestars, sea urchins, snapping shrimp, and spiny lobsters.

The *Monitor*'s remains are located near the northern boundary of tropical reef fish habitat and therefore support a mixture of temperate and tropical species. Fish abundance has been estimated by visual counts and verified from videotape from five transect lines over the length of the *Monitor*. Twenty-five species were observed (Table 2). The most abundant species was the red barbier. Thousands of fish, approximately 1.5 to 5 inches total length, formed schools at the stern and throughout the center of the vessel. The predominant predator species was the greater amberjack. Fifty-four fish were counted when approaching the *Monitor*. Approximately half of the wreck was visible so the number of jacks was estimated to be 108. Estimates of other common species included scad (several hundred); black sea bass (35); scup (14); bank sea bass (10); slippery dick (10); and vermilion snapper (6).

The *Monitor* has become a productive artificial reef. However, cold-water intrusions by the Labrador Current may limit its productivity. Several fish kills have been observed in the Cape Hatteras area since 1957. Reports indicate cold-water intrusion on the outer continental shelf may have contributed to the killing of red snapper and vermilion snapper. Most of the tropical species observed on the *Monitor* on past expeditions were juveniles or young adults.

Significant changes in the numbers and types of fish, corals and sponges have been noted over the years. Variations in the environment and even changes in the condition of the *Monitor*'s hull have been suggested as possible explanations.

Vessel Condition

During the years since the *Monitor* sank on December 31, 1862, its hull and contents have been slowly deteriorating. The *Monitor* sank at an offshore site where a hard seabed and strong currents have prevented the hull from becoming imbedded in a protective layer of sand and sediment. Also, the hull is partially suspended off the bottom by the displaced turret. As a result, there has been considerable structural damage and deterioration.

The *Monitor's* present condition is directly related to a combination of factors, including damage that occurred at the time of sinking, deterioration that has resulted from more than a century of immersion in a seawater environment, and possible damage from human activities. It has been theorized that depth-charging during World War II caused severe damage to the stern and lower hull. There is also evidence that the stern may have suffered serious damage in 1991 from one or more vessels anchoring on the *Monitor.* Fishing hooks and lines observed on the site during several NOAA and private expeditions suggest that fishing boats could be a source of continuing damage. However, most or all of the observable damage to the *Monitor's* hull may, in fact, be the direct result of natural deterioration.

The inverted hull of the *Monitor* rests on a nearly east-west orientation, partially submerged in bottom sediment with the port quarter supported by the displaced turret. The position of the turret under the port quarter armor belt and settling along the starboard armor belt caused by scouring action have combined to elevate the stern of the wreck and to produce an exaggerated list to starboard (south). In recent years, concerns have developed about the structural integrity of the port armor belt and deck, particularly about their ability to continue to support the port side. Detailed observations in 1987 failed to produce any indications of distortion or buckling in the port armor belt. Careful examination of the surface of the armor belt failed to locate distinct seams between armor belt plates, which would indicate that the plates were separating from each other or from the structure. However, in 1990, both NOAA and a private researcher observed several bulges in the armor belt that were interpreted by some as evidence of structural stress and by others merely as slight buckling of several plates.

The Hull

Analysis of data from several expeditions to the site indicates that the condition of the aft portion of the hull differs dramatically from the remains forward of midships. Along the sloping sides of the displacement hull, aft of the midships bulkhead, the plating has deteriorated, and many of the plates have fallen away. In some areas, only the iron frames remain. The distinctive skeg is visible, although displaced, as are the propeller and shaft. The shaft lies atop other displaced material beneath the stern, while the propeller lies atop structural material below and to port of its original position. The skeg has pulled completely free of the aft end of the lower hull and fallen off to starboard (south); each subsequent season finds that the skeg has shifted further.

The starboard quarter is buried to a depth of approximately five feet while the port quarter is supported more than seven feet above the bottom of the turret. Inside the hull, propulsion and auxiliary machinery appear to be collapsing toward the bottom sediment under the weight of the remains of the lower hull, which rests directly on the engineering space. Additional damage to the engineering space was caused by the displacement of the skeg and propeller shaft.

The midships bulkhead has partially collapsed, allowing the lower hull to settle down and to starboard. The twisted bulkhead frame is visible immediately forward of its original position, lying in the wreck atop displaced stanchions and the remains of hull plates. Much of the damage, including the loss of a number of plates from the port side and bottom of the lower hull, may be the result of recent anchoring incidents.

Forward of the midships bulkhead, deterioration of the lower hull is extensive. Although displaced sections of lower hull plating exist along the starboard side, no intact plating can be identified along the port side. Much of the material in evidence along the port side has been identified as portions of the interior of the ship, or equipment and fittings that were stowed below the crew's quarters, ward room, and galley. From the circular anchor well immediately aft of the bow, anchor chain leads over the starboard side and into the bottom sediments to the south.

Available data indicate that the destruction of the lower hull forward of the midships bulkhead closely resembles that which results from an explosion of considerable force. As the site is located in the traditional shipping lane off the North Carolina coast, it has been suggested that the damage is the result of the effects of depth charging during World War II. During the war, enemy submarines frequently rested on the continental shelf during the day, surfacing at night to destroy merchant ships along the coast. In an effort to prevent this, the Navy and the Coast Guard made a practice of dropping depth charges on all sonar targets. Quite possibly one of these targets was the *Monitor*. An explosion of this type in the area forward of the midships bulkhead would certainly have been capable of collapsing the already weakened hull of the vessel, and may also explain the distribution of hull plates upstream and a considerable distance from the *Monitor*. However, research at the site has revealed that strong currents can come from any direction and the observed deterioration may be due to natural causes.

The Deck

Bottom currents scour the seabed, altering the amount of exposed hull. Forward of the pilothouse, virtually all of the deck is usually suspended above the seabed and a portion of the pilothouse structure is exposed above the sediment. From this point aft to the turret, the entire port side of the vessel remains above the bottom, supporting its own weight and that of the sediment accumulated within the confines of the hull. Aft of the engineering space, the deck has suffered extensive damage and considerably less of the deck there supports itself. The armor plating on the deck has completely separated from the deck planking in several areas, indicating advanced deterioration.

At both the wardroom and midships locations where the deck of the *Monitor* is ruptured, material associated with the ship is washing out of the wreck and onto the sediment below. The amount of material redistributed in this manner appears to be augmented by pressure created by the current flowing over the wreck.

In the vicinity of the turret, deck plates have been dislodged by destruction associated with the stern of the vessel. Aft of the turret, sections of the deck have completely separated and armor plates hang suspended by deteriorated fittings. Forward of the turret, distinct separations between deck plates indicate that these plates are also separating from the wreck. Below the position of the port boiler uptake hatch, a portion of the smoke-pipe breaching is protruding from the deck and into the sediment.

The Turret

Structurally, the turret appears to be in good condition. The gunports are blocked by heavy wrought-iron port stoppers that protected the ordnance and gun crew from hostile fire. Wood bucklers that covered the gun ports while underway have not survived, although bolts that held them in place are intact and still protrude from the rammer holes in the port stoppers.

Shallow probing of the turret floor during NOAA's 1979 and 1993 expeditions verified that the turret deck (floor) has disintegrated. A hole in the deck above the turret has permitted silt and debris from inside the hull to fill the turret. Therefore, it is not possible to inspect the inside of the turret or to determine if the cannons are still in place.

Sanctuary Management

NOAA's management of the *Monitor* National Marine Sanctuary is designed to protect the site and its resources. NOAA conducts and permits scientific research on the *Monitor*. NOAA is also involved in a number of off-site management activities, including research and public education

The Mariners' Museum in Newport News, Virginia was selected in 1987 as the principal museum for curation of *Monitor*-related artifacts and papers and to cooperate with NOAA on a variety of educational projects, as described in the Administrative and Education sections of this plan.

Since designation of the site as a National Marine Sanctuary, access to the *Monitor* has been limited primarily to scientific research related to the vessel; however, special use permits make it possible to allow appropriate non-research activities. Prior to conducting on-site activities, a permit must be issued to NOAA pursuant to 15 CFR 924.5 (Appendix A). A summary of NOAA-permitted expeditions to the *Monitor* Sanctuary is included in Appendix B.

The current management structure for the *Monitor* National marine Sanctuary includes a manager and an education coordinator located in Tidewater Virginia. This staff reports to the Sanctuaries and Reserves Division, NOAA, in Silver Spring, Maryland.

Administration

Sanctuaries and Reserves Division

The National Marine Sanctuary Program is administered by NOAA's Sanctuaries and Reserves Division (SRD). A site-specific management plan is prepared for each individual sanctuary to ensure that resource protection, research, and education are coordinated and are consistent with National Marine Sanctuary goals and objectives.

SRD develops a general budget, setting out expenditures for program development, operating costs, and staffing. Funding priorities are reviewed and adjusted annually to reflect evolving conditions at the *Monitor* Sanctuary as well as National Marine Sanctuary Program priorities and requirements. SRD also establishes priorities and procedures in response to specific issues in each Sanctuary. Detailed SRD responsibilities are listed below in the Resource Protection, Research, and Education sections.

SRD National Programs

SRD's Technical Projects Branch provides a national focus for all sanctuary programs. This branch provides guidance on a wide variety of activities including research, education, resource management, damage response and assessment, and ecosystem health monitoring.

National program responsibilities for marine archaeology and maritime history reside within the SRD Technical Projects Branch. An Archaeologist/Historian fulfills NOAA's Federally-mandated responsibilities to advise the sanctuaries on cultural resource issues, to coordinate the issuance of permits for the disturbance of cultural resources (under section 106 of the National Historic Preservation Act, NHPA), and to inventory, evaluate and nominate to the National Register of Historic Places cultural resources within the sanctuaries (under Section 110 of the NHPA).

SRD produced an historical contexts study of the sanctuaries, "Fathoming Our Past," to identify potential resources and to educate sanctuary personnel about the importance of historical and cultural resources (Terrell 1994).

The SRD Archaeologist/Historian reviews all management plans, permit applications and other documents concerning the *Monitor* and provides other assistance as required. The Archaeologist/Historian also assists with the development of research designs and operations plans for on-site research.

Sanctuary Manager

The Sanctuary Manager for the *Monitor* reports directly to SRD in Silver Spring, Maryland. SRD is responsible for the overall management of the Sanctuary; however, the Sanctuary Manager is responsible for the day-to-day management of the site. The Manager represents SRD as a spokesperson for the *Monitor* Sanctuary.

Staffing

Minimum staffing for the *Monitor* Sanctuary is considered to be a full-time Sanctuary Manager and Education Coordinator. Those are currently the only two staff positions. Staffing could eventually include a Sanctuary Manager, an Office Manager, a Research Coordinator, an Education Coordinator, and one or more education and research assistants.

The Sanctuary staff works closely with the U.S. Coast Guard, other Federal and State agencies, and private organizations in order to provide for adequate site surveillance and enforcement, and to maintain active cooperative programs in research and education.

Sanctuary Headquarters

The Sanctuary's headquarters is located at The Mariners' Museum, Newport News, Virginia.

NOAA maintains a cooperative agreement with the United States Coast Guard (USCG) for enforcement of sanctuary regulations. The *Monitor* Sanctuary is within the USCG Fifth District, and Group Cape Hatteras directly assists NOAA with surveillance efforts and actions related to enforcing regulations at the *Monitor* Sanctuary.

Coast Guard units conduct surveillance during routine operations in the vicinity of the Sanctuary and also schedule periodic site inspections. Both air and surface craft are involved in surveillance activities. Group Cape Hatteras has provided excellent site coverage as well as support for research operations.

On September 4, 1986, NOAA published guidelines in the *Federal Register* for submitting proposals for consideration as principal museum for the *Monitor* Collection of Artifacts and Papers (now known as the *Monitor* Collection). After a thorough evaluation of all proposals, NOAA designated The Mariners' Museum, Newport News, Virginia, as the Principal Museum for the *Monitor* Collection. A Memorandum of Agreement between NOAA and the museum was signed on July 13, 1987 (Appendix C).

This agreement sets out the responsibilities of NOAA and The Mariners' Museum related to the *Monitor* Sanctuary. A programmatic cooperative agreement was signed between NOAA and The Mariners' Museum in October 1989. This agreement remains in effect until October 1999 and contains an option for renewal.

In the agreements, NOAA committed to:

- provide financial support for the services of the Mariners' Museum subject to annual appropriations, Federal law, and NOAA's approval;

- deliver to the Museum artifacts, papers, and records related to the *Monitor* NMS;

- provide funds to support base services and initiate special projects agreed to by the Museum and NOAA; and to designate a field manager for the *Monitor* Sanctuary to assist the Museum in implementing these agreements.

In the agreements, The Mariners' Museum committed to:

- maintain archives, a research library, and a conservation facility for the *Monitor*;

- develop permanent and traveling exhibits for the Sanctuary, and assist other participating museums in developing exhibits and interpretive displays;

- manage the lending of portions of the *Monitor* Collection to other qualified repositories for research, interpretation, or educational purposes;

- maintain the *Monitor* Collection under environmentally and physically secure conditions within storage, exhibition, laboratory, and study areas;

- inspect the *Monitor* Collection on a regular basis and make recommendations as to necessary maintenance conservation measures;

- adequately insure the *Monitor* Collection from theft and other loss;

- catalog all known *Monitor*-related materials in both private and public collections;

- assist and advise NOAA regarding the future planning of the *Monitor* NMS and development of the *Monitor* Collection;

- comply with relevant Federal regulations regarding the curatorship of Federally owned archaeological collections;

- provide other services relating to the *Monitor* NMS as agreed to by NOAA and the Museum.

Guidelines for use of the *Monitor* Collection by researchers are found in Appendix D.

U. S. Navy

Although the U. S. Navy officially abandoned the USS *Monitor* in 1953, the Naval Historical Center has maintained an active interest in the wreck, providing NOAA with comments and suggestions for historical and archaeological research. In 1993 the Naval Historical Center created a position for a nautical archaeologist who is developing a long-range program for management and research related to submerged U.S. Navy vessels and aircraft. The Center has been assisting NOAA with the development of management plans and research designs for the *Monitor* Sanctuary.

In addition, the U.S. Navy has actively participated in *Monitor* research beginning in 1974, with the R/V *Alcoa Seaprobe* expedition that mapped and confirmed the identity of the *Monitor*. Since that mission, the Navy has provided support for several research projects, including NOAA's *Monitor* Archaeological Research and Structural Survey (MARSS) in 1993 and, in 1995 a major cooperative project, the *Monitor* Archaseological Research, Recovery and Stabilization Mission (MARRS'95).

The U.S. Navy has agreed to participate with NOAA in future *Monitor* research on a non-interference basis, to the extent that equipment and personnel are available.

Other Public and Private Partners

Governmental Agencies

In 1991, NOAA established the Marine Historical Resource Evaluation Team (MHRET). The MHRET was chaired by NOAA, and its membership included the Chief Archaeologist from the Minerals Management Service, an archaeologist from the U.S. Department of the Interior; the Curator of Maritime History at the Smithsonian Institution; the Director of Maritime Preservation for the National Trust for Historic Preservation; and the Senior Historian of the U.S. Navy. The *Monitor* Sanctuary Manager and SRD obtained the MHRET's advice concerning resource management issues related to the *Monitor* Sanctuary. The MHRET reflected NOAA's ongoing efforts to solicit opinions from both the public and maritime-history professionals.

MHRET has been supplanted by an informal but larger and more diverse group of submerged cultural resource managers in the Washington, D.C. area that meets periodically and communicates regularly to discuss matters of concerns and to make recommendations when appropriate. NOAA's Maritime Historian/Archaeologist is a member of this group.

NOAA also obtains frequent assistance from the staffs of the North Carolina State Historic Preservation Office and the (Federal) Advisory Council on Historic Preservation who review and comment on permit applications for research at the Sanctuary, including NOAA-sponsored research.

Private Support

Over the years, a number of private organizations and individuals have provided valuable assistance to the *Monitor* Sanctuary. In 1990, for the first time, NOAA issued research permits to private dive groups who dove to the *Monitor* using conventional scuba equipment. Since then, the number of private research expeditions to the *Monitor* Sanctuary has increased dramatically, contributing photographs, video, computer-aided mapping and artifact recovery (See Appendix B).

NOAA is actively seeking to encourage and to participate with private researchers in attaining common research goals.

Education

- Recommends and provides to the SRD an annual educational priorities list and budget;

- Supervises the design/production of Sanctuary educational materials and facilities and provides training for educational staff;

- Encourages local and regional organizations to participate in Sanctuary education efforts;

- Oversees development of any education facilities constructed for the Sanctuary, reviews site analyses/design specifications, and makes recommendations on construction and maintenance contracts;

- Approves or denies Sanctuary education permits to ensure compliance with Sanctuary regulations;

- Issues education permits and oversees those activities.

The Education Coordinator:
- Develops and recommends the annual education plan to the Sanctuary Manager;

- Implements the education plan;

- Disseminates information to the public about the Sanctuary and the National Marine Sanctuary Program;

- With the Sanctuary Manager, makes presentations and produces written material for articles and educational packages;

- Maintains the *Monitor* Collection and serves as primary Sanctuary liaison to the Mariners' Museum.

The Sanctuaries and Reserves Division:

- Reviews and approves the list of annual priorities for education and the annual education budget prepared by the Sanctuary Manager;

- Reviews and approves design proposals for all educational facilities;

- Reviews and approves all educational materials prepared for the Sanctuary;

- Evaluates progress toward accomplishing objectives for education, and adjusts short- and long-term priorities accordingly.

Management

The Sanctuary Manager:

- Coordinates on-site efforts of all parties involved in Sanctuary activities;

- Identifies, analyzes, and resolves Sanctuary management problems and issues;

- Coordinates Sanctuary management with other Federal and State agencies and private organizations;

- Periodically reviews the management plan and recommends changes to the SRD;

- Prepares the annual Sanctuary budget and submits it to the SRD for approval;

- Oversees day-to-day Sanctuary operations, including administrative functions such as budgeting and purchasing activities;

- Represents Sanctuary viewpoints on local issues at public forums;

- Reviews and issues special-use permits.

The Sanctuaries and Reserves Division:

- Ensures that the Sanctuary is operated in a manner consistent with established National Program policies and with applicable national and international laws, and provides guidance to the Sanctuary Manager;

- Directs and assists the Sanctuary manager in implementing the Management Plan;

- Evaluates the effectiveness of Sanctuary management and regulatory measures;

- Reviews and approves a program budget for the Sanctuary submitted by the Sanctuary Manager;

- Provides funding for overall Sanctuary management and administration.

Resource Protection

Program Objectives

The *Monitor* National Marine Sanctuary was established in 1975 under the authority of Title III of the Marine Protection, Research, and Sanctuaries Act of 1972, as amended, (16 U.S.C. 1431 et seq.). Because of its national historical significance, the USS *Monitor* has also been placed on the National Register of Historic Places and designated a National Historic Landmark.

The primary purpose of the Management Plan is to provide a framework for the responsible protection and management of the *Monitor*, all associated artifacts, and the site itself. The Management Plan must also provide for resource protection in accordance with all applicable Federal laws. NOAA must insure that all proposed site activities comply with the regulations of the Marine Protection, Research and Sanctuaries Act; the Uniform Regulations for the Protection of Archaeological Resources; the National Historic Preservation Act (NHPA); and the National Environmental Policy Act (NEPA). In addition, all permit applications are submitted for review under the 36 CFR 106 review process, and approval is required by the Advisory Council on Historic Preservation. The Management Plan outlines several objectives for insuring the protection of the *Monitor* Sanctuary.

NOAA has identified four principal objectives for Resource Protection: public awareness, regulation enforcement, stabilization, and controlled artifact recovery.

Public Awareness

The first resource-protection objective is to promote public awareness of, and voluntary user compliance with, Sanctuary regulations through an education program stressing a resource conservation ethic and explaining the site's significance and fragile condition. Management experiences at the *Monitor* and other National Marine Sanctuaries have shown that the public must be made aware of the Sanctuary's location, significance, and activities that threaten the resource. An important aspect of managing the Sanctuary is to educate the diving, fishing, and boating public, and also those involved in related service industries (e.g., dive-boat operators, bait-and-tackle shops). This objective is further addressed in the Education section of this Management Plan.

Regulation Enforcement

The second resource protection objective is to maintain the current level of surveillance and enforcement. Through the agreement now in effect, the Sanctuary obtains regular U. S. Coast Guard assistance in enforcing Sanctuary regulations. If necessary, a Sanctuary enforcement officer may be added to the staff, funding permitting.

Stabilization

Previous NOAA studies indicated that the *Monitor* was deteriorating slowly. More recent studies, however, have shown that the hull has begun to deteriorate more rapidly. Therefore, NOAA is considering several options for stabilizing the *Monitor*, including cathodic protection and mechanical support. A 1987 study identified cathodic and anodic areas on the wreck where corrosion is occurring. One option currently being studied is to retard this corrosion process by installing cathodic protection on the hull. This system is similar to the method of attaching sacrificial anodes ("zincs") to the hulls of steel ships to retard galvanic action. Additionally, NOAA is studying the possibility of physically stabilizing the weakest portions of the structure, the armor belt and stern, through mechanical support such as jacks.

In-Situ Preservation

The fourth resource protection objective is to systematically recover artifacts when necessitated by any of the following situations:

- artifacts in danger of being damaged or destroyed due to natural elements (currents, corrosion, etc.);

- artifacts in danger of being damaged or destroyed due to deterioration or collapse of the vessel structure; or

- artifacts deemed important for scientific or archaeological studies or for exhibit.

In the context of this objective, the term "artifact" applies to components of the *Monitor*'s hull, as well as to machinery and contents.

Should theft and vandalism prove to be a significant problem at the site, additional artifact recovery could become necessary.

The option for complete recovery of the *Monitor*'s hull and contents was evaluated by NOAA during the past decade and eliminated for a variety of reasons. Data generated through on-site investigations by NOAA and private researchers indicate that the wreck has lost much of its structural integrity, particularly in the area aft of the midships bulkhead. The consensus of engineers and scientists who have worked at the site or reviewed the scientific data from the site is that any attempt at total recovery would result in extensive damage and/or destruction of major portions of the vessel and its contents.

While the technology exists to conserve the *Monitor*, should it be recovered, there is at present no facility capable of performing conservation on the entire hull or even major portions such as the turret. (The turret alone is more than 21 feet in diameter, 9 feet high and weighs in excess of 100 tons, not counting the two XI-inch Dahlgren cannons and other equipment currently entombed within it.) Furthermore, These factors, along with the exorbitant costs estimated for recovery and preservation (some estimates were in excess of $100 million), led NOAA to conclude that the recovery option was not viable.

In-situ preservation of the *Monitor* is the option most consistent with NOAA's general policy on historical and cultural resources, and with those of the Federal Archaeological Program. However, this option may no longer be appropriate for portions of the wreck and its contents that are threatened by hull collapse. As previously discussed, NOAA has studied various means of assisting *in-situ* preservation, including cathodic protection and physical stabilization.

Current On-site Activities

During the 1987 NOAA expedition, baseline corrosion measurements were taken at several hundred locations on the ship as a preliminary assessment of the potential for *in-situ* protection. However, NOAA's 1990 reconnaissance expeditions to the site documented changes in the vessel, including collapse of portions of the deck at the stern. These changes may render at least part of the 1987 data invalid, since shifts of structural material could have interrupted the electrical continuity that existed in 1987. Total cathodic protection would require comprehensive on-site investigations to reassess electrical conductivity. Limited cathodic protection at the turret-armor belt junction would require additional on-site data. Installation of the cathodic protection hardware would be a difficult and costly task, due to the difficult site environment.

Proposed On-site Activities

NOAA has reviewed several preliminary engineering proposals for physical stabilization of the hull, but no detailed plans have been generated due to limitations on funding. All of the proposed methods would be costly.

Other forms of *in-situ* preservation may be considered for the *Monitor* NMS. A diverse and imaginative suggestions have been made, including cofferdams, freezing, and underwater domes; however, these alternatives have not been fully evaluated.

Site inspection. Annual site assessments of the *Monitor* are conducted by NOAA and private researchers. NOAA prefers *in-situ* preservation, but exercises the option of recovering artifacts in danger of being lost or damaged. Conservation, preservation, interpretation and display of artifacts is accomplished through The Mariners' Museum.

NOAA-sponsored research. NOAA has sponsored or participated in a number of scientific research expeditions to the *Monitor* site, as outlined in Appendix B, and will continue to do so as funding permits.

Privately funded research. NOAA welcomes proposals from privately funded organizations for scientific research at the *Monitor* NMS. Proposals that comply with the guidelines included in this Management Plan have been approved and the resulting data and reports added to the growing body of information on the site. In 1991 NOAA actively sought proposals from outside sources through a notice in the *Federal Register*, and plans to continue and expand this policy. Since 1990, numerous private expeditions have conducted research dives and, under archaeological supervision, have recovered threatened artifacts.

NOAA-sponsored research. NOAA is developing a series of scientific research, engineering and recovery missions to the *Monitor* site as part of the ongoing long-range management plan. Possible objectives include completing research necessary to define the *Monitor*'s current condition; physically stabilizing portions of the *Monitor*'s hull; and mapping, recovering and conserving any artifacts and hull components determined to be in danger of damage or loss. Detailed operations plan will be prepared for each mission to address research needs, project goals, archaeological and engineering methodology, and artifact conservation and curation. NOAA will seek participation from public and private organizations for these missions, as appropriate.

Privately funded research. The level of private research at the *Monitor* NMS has increased markedly during the 1990s. As stated in the previous section, NOAA will continue to welcome and review proposals from privately funded organizations for scientific research at the *Monitor* NMS. It is expected that additional permits will be issued for privately funded research projects in the coming years, and that NOAA will participate in these projects to the fullest extent possible. NOAA is investigating various means for promoting cooperative research and assisting private groups in obtaining funding to support their activities.

Recreational access. Although protecting the resource is the most important management objective for the National Marine Sanctuary Program, NOAA also seeks to provide maximum access to the sanctuaries for the public's benefit and enjoyment. Based on its experience in managing the Sanctuary, and upon the non-research dives conducted during 1994, NOAA has determined that the *Monitor* can support limited access to divers for non-research purposes. This access will be controlled so as not to compromise the site's archaeological integrity or historical value. Restrictions have been established to protect the resource. A special-use permit will be required, which identifies and conditions the allowed/prohibited activities during the visit. On-board observers are an option for all NOAA-permitted activities. NOAA will implement this policy through the issue of a special use permits to a concessionaire who will be responsible for planning and scheduling the dives, establishing diver qualification criteria and conducting the dives. This revised access policy recognizes the expressed interest in increased public access to the sanctuary, while still carrying out NOAA's mandate under the MPRSA to protect this national historic resource.

Unlimited access. NOAA does not consider unlimited access to the sanctuary to be an acceptable option due to the high probability of adverse impact from anchors, debris, or other material intentionally or unintentionally coming into contact with the wreck. Comments on the draft revised management plan indicated general support for controlled access to the *Monitor*.

Mooring system. NOAA has installed two underwater mooring systems to assist site research and visitation. A small mooring with a subsurface buoy can be located and used by divers for a descent/ascent line. A larger mooring, located 500 feet southwest of the *Monitor*, can accommodate a small diving support vessel and is available for use by permitted activities. The buoy for this mooring is located at a depth of 50 feet. Surface buoys are not used, since they would be expensive to maintain and would pose a hazard to navigation.

Research

Program Objectives

Sanctuary research projects funded by SRD will generally address the resolution of management issues and concerns. The Sanctuary Manager and SRD staff will follow research selection procedures established by SRD to ensure that the Sanctuary's research program is consistent with the policies and directions of the National Marine Sanctuary Program. Research selection procedures include preparing an annual Sanctuary Research Plan and reviewing applications for research submitted by other organizations, both private and governmental.

Since 1977, research at the *Monitor* site has been directed toward documenting the wreck in detail and understanding how it has been affected by natural deterioration and human activities. Since research itself may result in harm to the resource, or increase the risk of harm, all research conducted at the *Monitor* site is subject to the Sanctuary's permit regulations, to the SRD's permit guidelines (see Appendices A and E), and all applicable Federal historic preservation legislation.

In 1987, NOAA completed baseline studies at the site that are essential for determining the rate of deterioration of the hull and changes in the Sanctuary environment. In 1990 and 1991, NOAA conducted site inspection studies to document changes in the *Monitor* and its immediate environment.

General research goals for the Sanctuary are the continued scientific recovery and dissemination of historical and cultural information preserved at the site, the continued scientific study of the *Monitor* as an artificial reef, and the careful review and monitoring of privately-sponsored research activities in order to ensure that the site is protected and preserved and that the research results will make the maximum contribution to the overall data base.

Research Objectives

Research is essential to the acquisition of data that contribute directly to the resolution of management, interpretation, protection, and preservation issues in the *Monitor* Sanctuary. This section outlines research topics and tasks that yield data of the highest priority. Anyone interested in developing alternative proposals is encouraged to seek technical assistance from NOAA. At the present time, NOAA will encourage and give highest priority to research proposals that contribute to responsible-option assessments and yield the following types of information:

- Trends data generated through predictive studies designed to assess causes and effects of corrosion, environmental conditions, and human activities;

- Engineering data that will permit accurate assessment of the potential for stabilizing the *Monitor*'s hull *in situ* through cathodic protection, mechanical support or other means;

- Historical data generated through archival records and on-site investigation to enable development of a comprehensive depiction of the *Monitor* as the vessel existed on December 31, 1862;

- Archaeological data that contribute to developing an adequate model of the nature and disposition of the wreck and its associated artifacts through application of systematic principles of underwater archaeology;

- Engineering studies to determine missing design and construction details on the vessel,

- Engineering studies to determine the best methods of deploying equipment and personnel on deepwater archaeological sites, and development of predictive models on the effects of alternative recovery methods for the wreck or its selected features;

- Conservation data to identify preservation problems with the wreck *in situ* and to develop predictive models on the problems encountered with recovery, stabilization and display of the wreck and its associated artifacts;

- Biological studies of the *Monitor* as a living artificial reef of exact known age.

In order to promote the development of research proposals for the *Monitor* Sanctuary, the following examples have been included to suggest a variety of research topics and needed information:

- *Study topic:* On-site engineering and structural data collection. *Information needs:* Annual resource assessment to determine changes occurring on the wreck structure due to natural deterioration and/or human impact. Recovery of small, endangered artifacts that may have been dislodged from the wreck.

- *Study topic:* Analysis of water conditions and sea state. *Information needs:* A survey of the existing weather and environmental records pertaining to the Hatteras area and the development of a comprehensive model of the annual weather conditions as an aid to on-site research.

- *Study topic:* Study of currents, visibility, erosion, depositional patterns, and the nature of the water column in the *Monitor* Sanctuary. *Information needs:* An environmental definition of the *Monitor* site is necessary for two reasons. First, to determine the effect of the environment on the wreck and, second, to assist in planning and conducting on-site research. The deployment and maintenance of current meter arrays, the collection of water column analysis data (e.g., salinity, temperature, depth (STD), oxygen content, suspended particulate matter) and the collation of these data will assist in determining the conditions encountered during on-site archaeological research. This study was initiated in 1990 with the deployment of a thermistor to record water temperature.

- *Study topic:* Surface and subsurface sediment studies. *Information needs:* Analysis of the character of sediments will assist in interpreting sediment deposition and archaeological site formation.

- *Study topic:* Continued site definition. *Information needs:* Locate and identify material associated with the wreck but existing outside the confines of the hull remains.

- *Study topic:* On-site test excavations. *Information needs:* Evaluate the nature and extent of the archaeological record. Test excavations both inside and outside the confines of the hull could generate archaeological, engineering and environmental data that would expand knowledge of the wreck site and its environment.

- *Study topic:* Develop a plan for conservation, curation and exhibit of material recovered from the site for each of the following options: (a) continued limited collection of small artifacts; (b) selected recovery of portions of the wreck and its contents. *Information needs:* Detailed conservation and exhibit plan, including necessary procedures, facilities, budget, etc.

- *Study topic:* Conduct a photogrammetric analysis of existing stereo photography. *Information needs:* To generate horizontal and vertical profiles and produce an accurate photomosaic of the wreck site. (This was initiated in FY91.)

- *Study topic:* Corrosion studies. *Information needs:* Data generated by electric field gradient measurements, structure-to-structure electrolyte potential measurements, and other tests to assist in evaluating the potential for *in-situ* preservation.

- *Study topic:* Physical *in-situ* support of the stern of the wreck. *Information needs:* As weakening of the port armor belt may cause the stern to collapse, options for physically supporting and stabilizing the portion of the stern presently supported by the turret should be considered.

- *Study topic:* Contingency plans for collapse of the port armor belt. *Information needs:* Because the port armor belt, one of the primary support members for that side of the wreck, is exhibiting signs of stress, a contingency plan for the recovery, conservation, curatorship, and display of the turret and/or other portions of the vessel that are of special interest should be developed.

- *Study topic:* Archival research of World War II records relative to depth-charging activities in the vicinity of the *Monitor.* *Information needs:* Documentation verifying that the remains of the *Monitor* were depth-charged during World War II would enhance our understanding of the site and of the extensive damage that has occurred at the stern of the wreck.

- *Study topic:* Archival research of additional *Monitor* data. *Information needs:* Papers relating to the *Monitor*'s inventor, John Ericsson, have not all been catalogued; other papers in public and private repositories might be identified and added to the *Monitor* archives.

Program Elements

Annual Research Plan

The *Monitor* National Marine Sanctuary will prepare and update a five-year Sanctuary Research Plan from which annual research plans will be developed. The annual research planning process for the Sanctuary will involve the following steps:

- Sanctuary management concerns will be identified, with supporting evidence and rationale;

- Research priorities consistent with the Sanctuary's goals will be established, based upon research needs and management concerns; *and*

• From the above information detailed research plan and operations plan will be developed.

Research priorities will be recommended by the Sanctuary Manager to the SRD headquarters staff and draft research and operations plans presented for review and approval.

Important factors to be considered in establishing research priorities include immediate or evolving management issues which can be resolved through directed research and prospects of related research in progress.

Following SRD headquarters' approval of the Sanctuary's annual Research Plan, the plan will be incorporated into the National Marine Sanctuary Program's Research Plan for the year. If appropriate, announcements of research needs will be made and requests for proposals issued. Announcement and requests for proposals will discuss identified management concerns and summarize past and current related research. Approval and funding of research proposals are the responsibility of SRD and the Sanctuary.

As funds become available, NOAA will conduct research at the *Monitor*. The Sanctuary Manager will also work with independent researchers with private funds who are interested in conducting research at the site. Research selection procedures will be those established by SRD for the overall National Marine Sanctuary Program to ensure that the *Monitor* Sanctuary's research program is consistent with the policies and directions of the National Program.

As a routine activity, the Sanctuary Manager will monitor the performance of researchers conducting research activities at the Sanctuary. The Manager will maintain records of all current research equipment being used on-site, the frequency of researchers' visits to the site, and current progress on each project. Interim progress reports by the researchers will be reviewed by the Sanctuary Manager to ensure adherence to the terms of the research permit. Final research reports maybe reviewed by scientists recognized in a particular field of research, as well as by resource managers, before final approval of the report the Sanctuary Manager and SRD headquarters.

Education

Program Objectives

The purpose of the education program is to enhance public awareness and understanding of the Sanctuary's significance and the need to protect this vital historic resource. This section describes specific program objectives and educational products.

Public Awareness

Expanding public awareness involves four primary aims: promoting a general understanding of the National Marine Sanctuary Program; bringing the *Monitor* to the public; enhancing the understanding of the natural and man-made processes affecting the *Monitor*; and enhancing the understanding of the diversity of marine life inhabiting the *Monitor* Sanctuary. A discussion of each of these aims follows.

Promoting a general understanding of the National Marine Sanctuary Program.

This can be achieved by:

• Including National Marine Sanctuary Program material in mailings of *Monitor* Sanctuary information and as part of public programs and presentations on the *Monitor* Sanctuary.

• Depicting the *Monitor* Sanctuary as part of a national program in exhibits and displays.

• In cooperation with other sanctuary education coordinators, developing joint education products focusing on two or more sanctuaries to emphasize the diversity of resources encompassed by the National Marine Sanctuary Program.

Bringing the Monitor *to the public.*

This can be achieved by:

• Developing a wide variety of materials, including brochures, posters, publications, slide and video programs, and presentations on the value of the *Monitor* as a National Marine Sanctuary and as a significant historic vessel.

• Sponsoring special events and programs designed to present various aspects of the *Monitor* National Marine Sanctuary and to encourage public participation.

• Participating in programs, special events, and other forums developed and sponsored by other agencies or organizations by providing presentations and/or displays on the *Monitor* National Marine Sanctuary.

Enhancing the understanding of the natural and man-made processes affecting the **Monitor.**

This can be achieved by:

- Developing a variety of products geared to the public—including elementary, middle, and high school students—that promote the understanding of the significance and present condition of the *Monitor* and the need to preserve it.

- Developing products to reach special- interest groups, including fishermen and sport divers, to provide current information on regulations and policy decisions, and to promote the *Monitor*'s preservation.

- Developing products geared to the professional community to solicit information about current research on other wrecks that may be applicable to preserving the *Monitor*.

Enhancing the understanding of the diversity of marine life inhabiting the **Monitor** *Sanctuary.*

This can be achieved by:

- Incorporating current information on marine life into programs and presentations on the *Monitor*.

- Developing displays and exhibits that promote information and stimulate interest in the *Monitor* as an artificial reef.

- Continuing to work with marine biologists to update the list of marine life documented at the site as part of every expedition report or summary.

Research and Archives

There are two primary objectives for research and archives:

Maintaining the **Monitor** *Collection currently curated by* ***The Mariners' Museum in Newport News, Virginia.***

This can be achieved by:

- Continuing to archive research data as it is generated, and making it available to the public.

- Continuing to archive papers from NOAA, other agencies, and individuals involved in *Monitor*- related activities as they become available, and making them available to the public.

- Soliciting donations of *Monitor*-related material from the private sector.

- Producing annual supplements to the *Monitor* Collection catalog.

Promoting interpretation and display of **Monitor***-related artifacts and research materials in diverse geographic areas.*

This can be achieved by:

- Developing plans for interpreting and displaying artifacts recovered from the Sanctuary to ensure that the public has access to them in exhibits.

- Developing traveling exhibits and displays on various aspects of the *Monitor* Sanctuary, including the vessel's history, on-site research, current management directions, and marine life found on the wreck.

- Providing such material as documents, photographs, slides and videotapes to museums, educational institutions, and public and private organizations wishing to develop *Monitor*-related displays or exhibits.

- Working with the Mariner's Museum and other maritime museums to develop workshops that utilize *Monitor*-related products in ways that stimulate interest in the *Monitor*, the National Marine Sanctuary Program, and cultural and natural resources.

Encouraging the use of the **Monitor** *Collection for school papers, theses, dissertations, and special studies projects.*

This can be achieved by:

- Developing ongoing internship programs in conjunction with one or more high schools and/or universities. The programs will emphasize the fields of museum studies, maritime history, cultural resource management, underwater archaeology, and science.

- Notifying museums, educational institutions, and the public of the *Monitor* Collection's availability and diversity.

- Issuing periodic announcements of new data acquisitions to the *Monitor* Collection.

Education Products

Media

Information Booklet: The booklet *A Look at the* Monitor *National Marine Sanctuary: Past, Present and Future* provides a concise history of the *Monitor*, the Sanctuary, and an overview of research and education activities.

Monitor *National Marine Sanctuary Brochure.* This illustrated color brochure conforms to SRD standards and includes site location, regulations, and general information about the Sanctuary.

Paper Model. This attractive, accurate cutout model is designed for children at the third-grade level and above. It is an easy-to-assemble model with instructions and supplemental information about the *Monitor* Sanctuary. The model is available at no cost to school systems.

Cheesebox. *Cheesebox*, an activities report for the Sanctuary, is produced and distributed annually. *Cheesebox* is written for a general audience and contains current information on *Monitor*-related issues and activities including on-site research, exhibits, management issues, and historical notes.

Poster. A four-color poster that conforms to SRD standards is available for the *Monitor* Sanctuary. This poster is intended to provide information on the *Monitor* and to promote a heightened awareness of the ship and the Sanctuary.

Traveling Exhibit for North Carolina. This traveling exhibit details the history and sinking of the *Monitor*, the wreck's discovery, and current management and on-site research. Although the exhibit was developed primarily for North Carolina museums, it has already traveled to facilities in other states. The exhibit includes photographs, a model of the *Monitor*, and a video.

Comprehensive Bibliography. This ongoing effort will result in a bibliography with periodic supplements consisting of primary and secondary sources (e.g., news articles, papers, and monographs). The bibliography will be available by June 1996.

List of Available Materials. This is a list of publications, videos, brochures, posters, and other materials available to the public. It is updated as necessary and distributed in information packages, as part of presentations and programs on the *Monitor*, and to contacts within school systems for history, science, and related courses of study.

Curricula/Special Presentations

Curriculum Development. *Monitor* Sanctuary staff, Mariners' Museum education staff, and educators from the Virginia public school system have developed a curriculum for use in history and science classes. The curriculum targets seventh grade and will be expanded gradually to develop units for middle and high schools.

Internship Program. Continuing internship programs have been developed in conjunction with local high schools. Students interested in museum studies, maritime history, cultural resource management, underwater archaeology, and science are encouraged to participate. Internship programs will also be developed with area universities.

Narrated Video. Since most of the scientifically-valuable data generated by on-site research is on videotape, a 20-minute narrated video will be developed in-house to be used as an adjunct to presentations by *Monitor* Sanctuary and headquarters staff. Supplemental handouts will facilitate use of the video as an educational tool. The video will be available by June 1996.

Products for Younger Children. A children's book is planned that discusses the *Monitor*'s significance, John Ericsson's importance as an inventor, the *Monitor-Virginia* battle, the sinking, the wreck's discovery, National Marine Sanctuary designation, and on-site research.

Illustrated with black-and-white sketches or line drawings, the book will be reviewed by educators and test-marketed with at least two groups of children before final production.

Exhibits Catalog: To better assist museums and other facilities interested in developing exhibits on the *Monitor,* an exhibits catalog will be produced. It will contain photographs of artifacts recovered from the *Monitor* that are available for exhibit, graphics, and examples of still images of the wreck. It will also contain instructions on how to apply for a loan of artifacts.

Special Events. Sanctuary staff will develop concepts for, and also participate in, special *Monitor*-related events. "*Monitor* Day" events are held throughout the calendar year at The Mariners' Museum and include re-enactors representing Union and Confederate soldiers and sailors, interpreters who discuss life aboard the *Monitor*, and Civil War music.

Public Presentations. Sanctuary staff will present programs, as logistically and financially feasible, on the *Monitor* National Marine Sanctuary upon request to professional meetings, special-interest groups, public-service organizations, educational institutions, and other events.

Cooperative Projects

Cooperative Projects with the Mariner's Museum. Under the current Memorandum of Agreement between NOAA and the Mariner's Museum, specific cooperative education projects and products will be identified and developed by the museum's Education Division and the Sanctuary Education Coordinator. These include:

- ***Interpreter.*** A professional interpreter is present one day a week to interpret life aboard the *Monitor* for museum visitors. Special interpretive programs are developed for events as well as for the holidays, including Christmas.

- ***Paper Model.*** This will be designed for children at the third-grade level and above. It will be an easy-to-assemble model with supplemental information about the *Monitor* Sanctuary. The model will be available to school systems and for use in workshops to be developed by the Mariner's Museum.

- ***Exhibits for the Cape Hatteras area.*** Three specific products will be developed in an effort to expand education outreach in the Cape Hatteras area. The first will be laminated copies of the Sanctuary regulations, which will be offered to fishermen and distributed in marinas, restaurants, fish houses, and bait shops. The second will be a wayside exhibit near the ferry terminal to provide information on the Sanctuary, including regulations, to tourists and local residents. The third will be a long-term photographic display placed in the community center or library to provide information on current *Monitor*-related activities.

- *Narrated Slide Program.* This program will be offered to schools and public-service organizations to provide current information on management directions, on-site research, and *Monitor*-related activities. The program will be updated periodically to reflect new research data and current activities.

- *"Touch Screen" Program.* The concept for this sophisticated education program will be developed over several years. This product will utilize state-of-the-art electronic media to allow people to interact with computerized programs as they learn about the *Monitor* Sanctuary.

- *Monitor **Model**.* This will be a three-dimensional model, probably constructed of wood, that can be disassembled and reassembled to encourage hands-on activities in discussing the vessel's construction and the *Monitor*'s significance to naval history.

- ***Workshops.*** Cooperative workshops will include a simulated dive on the *Monitor* for school children, using the video generated by on-site research. Other workshops will incorporate the three-dimensional and paper models of the *Monitor*.

Cooperative Projects with Other National Marine Sanctuaries. Products may include posters with a regional focus, such as Atlantic and Great Lakes Region sanctuaries, or a combination of sanctuaries selected to illustrate the diversity of resources included in the sanctuary program. Posters would include information on the sanctuaries and a contact for obtaining additional information. Other products with a regional focus could include summaries of research with a general rather than technical focus, and a compendium of information including history, significance, access, and regulations.

Appendices

Appendix A: Final Regulations

Appendix B: NOAA-Permitted Expeditions

Appendix C: Cooperative Agreement

Appendix D: Mariners' Museum: Use of the Collection

Appendix E: Permit Guidelines: Archaeological Research

Appendix F: Permit Guidelines: Research and Education

Appendix G: NOAA-Sponsored Publications

Note: All appendices contain out of date and/or inaccurate information and were not included in this text document.

John Broadwater, ONMS, 12 February 2009

www.ingramcontent.com/pod-product-compliance
Lightning Source LLC
Chambersburg PA
CBHW080354290526
45791CB00009BA/2866